First edition December 2020

ISBN 978-0-5788-1575-6

From the Dog Shelter *to the* White House

THE STORY OF MAJOR BIDEN

KALEA MARTIN and KENNEDI RIANNE

My name is Major Biden, and today I'm moving into the White House.

Rex Reagan

Millie & Ranger Bush

BUDDY & SOCKS CLINTON

BARNEY BUSH

BO & SUNNY OBAMA

CHAMP & MAJOR BIDEN

That's me!

Before I met Joe and Jill,
I was living at the
Delaware Humane
Association.

I didn't have a family,
and I felt lonely all the time.

The best part of the day was when people visited the shelter.

“Will they be my new family?”
I wondered as people walked by.

I waited and waited.

I worried and I worried.

I hoped and hoped.

I'm going home today!

You said that yesterday.

Finally the day came.
Ashley Biden found me,
and she told her parents,
Joe and Jill.

When I met Joe and Jill,
they petted me over and over again.

"We're gonna be alright,"

Joe told me.

And he was right.
The day that Joe and Jill adopted me
was the best day of my whole life.

At home, I got all the love, care, and attention that I waited so long for.

I got to meet my brother Champ,
who is also a German Shepherd,

I got to eat a big dinner,

CHAMP

MAJOR

and I got to play with
Joe and Jill's grandchildren.

I have a happy life now,
thanks to Joe and Jill.

And now I get to share my favorite humans with the rest of America.

Today we're moving
into the White House.

The End.

From the Dog Shelter to the White House is the debut children's book o
Kalea Martin and Kennedi Rianne.
Both are professional creatives and
dog lovers based out of Arizona.

CPSIA information can be obtained
at www.ICGtesting.com
Printed in the USA
LVHW072222190221
679377LV00026B/339

* 9 7 8 1 0 8 7 9 4 3 3 8 1 *